HANGING OUT IN THE QUIET

POEMS & THE STORIES BEHIND THEM

ARLENE McGUIRE

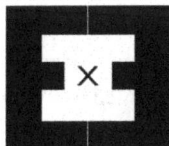

EXPECTED END

X

ENTERTAINMENT

ATLANTA, GA

DEDICATION

This book is dedicated to my grandmother, Muriel Gray, and my mother, Thelma Markland.

CONTENTS

PREFACE   i

1 Ode to Mom   1

2 Ode to Dad   7

3 Belief   13

4 Holding Hands 17

5 The Grand Grands 21

6 A Girl   25

7 A Boy   29

8 For Love's Sake 35

9 Fight for Love   39

10 Are You Alone 43

11 Go Fish for Your Life 47

12 Dance of a Young and Old Soul 51

13 I Thought You Knew 57

14 He Man   61

15 The Unexpected 65

16 Day's End   69

CONTENTS

17   Hanging Out in the Quiet   73

18   Vision   79

19   Handkerchief   83

20   Dreams of Youth   87

21   Haiku Poems   93

22   Short Verses   99

23   Love Scene   107

24   A Bad ED Day   111

25   A Bad ED Night   115

26   A Personal Sexual Revolution: Sex After ED   119

27   A Touching Encounter   123

28   Awaiting the New Year   127

29   No Sun   133

30   Instead   137

31   Men's Poem   141

32   Prayer   145

PREFACE

Metal striking metal or a twig rubbing a twig eventually causes a spark that will bring a flame. That flame fanned a little while brings a full burn and that is exactly how this book began.

Lack in my life kept the desire to do something gnawing at the back of my mind. The lack of education is the weakness I feel most. It has held me back for most of my life. The feeling of inadequacy robbed me of the belief that I could compete.

With age, that sometimes dissipates. It did for me. All I could think about was producing something that would say I was here. The day-to-day became more pleasant as I dreamed of many scenarios of what I could accomplish.

I had to put the dream into action because the years were not waiting for me. So, I began the search of what it would take to write a book. After reading a lot of articles, I gave up that idea. Then I decided to look at being a motivational speaker. Yes, I realized that would be quite a challenge. But in that seminar, I met someone who had the information I needed. Yes, I was back to the book idea, in full force.

Today, you are reading a dream come true. I have accomplished one more great thing in life. The other things of greatness are three wonderful children I was blessed with. Now they have blessed me with six equally wonderful grandchildren.

I hope this book makes you smile. I hope this book makes you challenge yourself about something you should do.

If you have done all you can to date, maybe there is one more thing you should do.

Look in the hat, check up your sleeve for the rabbit. There may be someone waiting on the smile your accomplishment will bring.

Just read this work for fun, nothing more.

1
ODE TO MOM

ODE TO MOM

My life took you by surprise
but you chose life for me
only to find yours cut in half
by an incapacitating handicap.
How does a mother care for a child with one hand?
Who can prepare a 21-year-old
newly wedded woman for that?
I cannot imagine how you survived the shock
and pain of these life-changing events.
But you stood tall and faced it all.
May I say you did it your way,
often with help from a friend.
Your mother became my mother
and we moved through this life in different places,
yet we knew the love of each other.

I have often wondered where we would be,
how different we would be if you were my mother.
As the years followed each other, the distance ebbed and
flowed until our final few years arrived.
We found a sense of mother and child in our old age.
We found the depth that was missing in our hugs.
We found our tears mingled as we laughed
at your sillies or mine.
Best of all, we found the Joy and Peace
of our Creator as we shared prayer.

Now you are asleep in Him.
Your years of service are accounted for.
Your wings are on and your feet are shod
for walking all over His Heaven with you mother.

I have gone past missing you both.
I have replaced the sadness with a smile.

You see, I am clear on the event that awaits me now.
At that time, you will be there with welcoming arms,
but today my heart is full
of Love for the life you saved, mom.
I face the tasks and shoulder the burdens
as I watched you do,
feeling happy to be alive
and remembering you.
I Love you MOM!

STORY BEHIND "ODE TO MOM"

August of 2012, I took my mother to the emergency room. She stayed in the hospital for the next five months until she left us and went home.

Today, I find myself waving to her as I pass the Floral Hills Resting Gardens where she sleeps. My visits with her always leave me feeling refreshed. I was always being silly when I was with her, and I still talk and joke with her.

It was such a backward life we led... apart in my infancy, full on war as a teenager, and totally rebellious as a young adult and a very needy adult.

Mother went through all these phases with me with prayer. All the drama and trauma I showed up with did not cause a misstep with her other three daughters.

We had a good laugh once as she explained that she wore a different hat with each of her children. Now when I am in one of those hat-change modes, that memory makes me smile.

I stayed amazed at my mother for most of my life after I got over my bad behaviors.

To see all that she accomplished with only one arm often causes me to be upset with some people who allow their handicap to defeat them.

She was vibrant and always living life to the fullest. There were the grandchildren to see about and then the great grandchildren. Oh, the joy she experienced with our children. As her mother did before her, she did not miss birthdays, or prayer time, when the opportunity presented themselves.

Like her mother before her, we had awesome examples

of what a mother and father rolled up into one looked like.

As the firstborn, I am sure I caused her the most pain. Watching your child bump their head repeatedly is very difficult. I can attest to that now. I can tell you I know what she felt because I had the opportunity with my own three children.

We laughed with the "I told you so" and the "your turn to suffer" and the "just like her mother" comments.

I lived with these two ladies and was so blessed by their lives that words cannot express. But this poem for my mom was a small effort.

2
ODE TO DAD

ODE TO DAD

As a child, I saw you as a very tall tower
I know that the tower disappeared
never to be found again, then the quest began
in each male that crossed my path
I searched for you, your smile, your feeling of security
in someone else's arms

How long do I hold on to the hope that one day you will
return
The years go by and not one single word, but I just keep on
loving you, especially because folks keep saying how much
I look like you
I would like to see it for myself, so I dream and dream...

Have you any idea how seeing you way down the years of
my life felt
Have you any idea how I wanted you to wave a magic
wand and erase all the sadness
Being with you and my mom for that brief moment in time
made me the most happy human on the planet

But that time was short lived and the unforgiveness we
harbored came into being
Yes, we made new memories but they were not strong
enough to support the life ahead
The past collided with the present and resentment won each
trial
How easily you gave up on me
It was of no importance to make up for lost years
Did my need for you in my life not outweigh your new
family
The love for you made my heart beat so much faster
but your drums could not listen to mine so apart again was
easy now

Our assurance in the fact that we knew we would not make
it in the first place
You made me, you left me
You found me, you left me
Now, all I have is a conglomeration of sad and happy
memories, memories that are unfinished, memories that are
more painful than angry now

Your trials were great and you weathered the storms of life
I believe we will meet again and we will get it right in that
reunion
Sleep finally arrived for you and I wish you sweet rest in
peace.

STORY BEHIND "ODE TO DAD"

Now I lay me down to sleep I pray the Lord my soul to keep
If I should die before I awake
I pray the Lord my soul to take
Please bless Mommie, Daddy and brother and sister.......
Amen

You were more than likely taught this poem or a similar one by a parent. Hooray for granny, who taught me all the prayers I know. I lived with my dad for a short time twice in my life at age seven and age 30. More than likely he did not even know these prayers.

So, I must admit that I feel that lack even now as an adult. It's great to see fathers putting children to bed.

That reminds me of some of the childhood songs we sang for example:

Rock a bye baby on the tree top
when the wind blows the cradle will rock
if the bow breaks the cradle will fall
down comes the baby the cradle and all

I am sure many readers will know this prayer. You may have even said this prayer when you were a small child. I found joy in it because I played the child's innocence and the grownup cynical side shined through.

I have seen a few takes on other childhood poems or sayings or prayers, if you will, and found them to be funny. One example is the movie, *The Hand that Rocks the Cradle*. That's not how I viewed the caring person taking care of a baby. Then there's humpty dumpty, showing that egg all broken was horrible to me. The best one is the song, Rock a Bye Baby. Now, the face of the baby in that picture had me dying. That baby wanted that caregiver to know that he was not happy about this song. What wind? Why am I out in the wind anyway?

I had the most fun thinking about that song in that way, hence my take on this poem.

Now, this is a poem the two smallest grandchildren have been taught. I may be miles away but sometimes I call to say, "Don't forget to say your prayers."

When I was very young, I was very sad because prayers were prohibited in our schools.

Because I grew up in the church and attended a school affiliated with my church, all I knew was church. Saying prayers in a new school and a new country was very comforting to me. Then they took it away. Politically, I had no clue and could have cared less what it meant. All I knew is I missed that time.

My new family was not religious so Sunday School and all the other church activities I knew was missing from my life.

I had all those prayers memorized so I could still feel the comfort they brought. This was a very scary place and I could comfort myself at night with my prayers. That is a huge part of why the youngest grands are taught a few of these prayers.

It's not about religion; it's simply a way to help them believe they are not alone, that someone loves them and will help them. For those who disagree with that working premise, I understand. However, I look at how a child's simplicity and a grownup's view of the same prayer differ. But as adults, we can still say that simple childlike prayer and feel whole, safe and heard. The little ones haven't quit grasped the feeling that their prayers have been heard.

Dad, I am so sorry you were not there to share this life-long memory of children's prayers and nursery rhymes with me.

I still love you so much dad.

3
BELIEF

BELIEF

Did you ever believe in me
The goal of a union is to achieve
Complete trust in each other
It should be the most important consideration from the
beginning
Testing the ability of an acquaintance for truth
The passing of time carries the toll card
Which gives the final determination of the matter
The day the most dark event of life
Spreads its wings over you
You do not want to be in doubt
You do not want to think twice
You want to close your eyes
With a certainty that you believe
You believe in that person and what you believe you know
to be truth
You have tried them with fire and they have been golden
So now in the darkness of this fragile experience
You can rise from those ashes
From the debris of doubt
Because as you stand and lift up your head
As you throw off the dusty cloak of gloom and pain
As you throw back your head and look down the road of
your life
The truth rises with you
That ray of sunshine shines out from the recesses of your
heart
And you know that you believe
You believe that you are loved

STORY BEHIND "BELIEF"

Belief was written from a very dark place in my life. By now you can tell that I have very many dark places. If you know me, you know that those dark places, times and experiences have not totally tainted me. I still love laughter, love to be silly and best of all, I love life. The folks who put me through the hard tasks have had the opportunity over the years to talk about it with me and to our amazement, we find common ground where pain is what we sometimes need to see the truth.

This poem spoke volumes to my pain. I needed assurances that my worth was important. I needed to feel that I was trying to prove that nothing could shake my resolve.

As I write this, I remind myself of the other idea, word or feeling I need to write about... Loyalty. It kind of goes hand-in-hand with belief, in the fact that the emotion one feels is worthy and reciprocated. All these are encompassed in the staunchness of loyalty.

Weathering the harsh truths of what one believes is a daunting task sometimes, or should I say most of the time. But when those challenges arrive, we fight our way through the blinding darkness and finally arrive on the other side. Eventually, we come out on the other side with sound understanding of yet another lesson.

I did come through that darkness much better because I learned a deeper meaning of belief. I had to rewrite the whole idea of my earlier understanding of belief and adjust the life meter and begin again.

It was at this time in my life that I needed to reevaluate some outdated ideas and revisit the bars I had set for my life. Some were too high, others not high enough. Some were totally displaced. It took this moment to stop me to make me take charge and change.

We can put our pain to good use by using it to change.

4
HOLDING HANDS

HOLDING HANDS

When you held my hand, it brought me so much joy.
Your clasping fingers sent a strong message of security,
As if you were putting an invisible cloak around me.
It would pull me closer to your side.
I could feel the strength of your stride
While following the directions to my wrist.
Move left or move right, now a quick motion that says
Let's stop for a moment and let this throng go by.
Pulling me close now, we move into a sheltering doorway,
Into a warming embrace.
My hand is free now and feeling so small.
In your eyes, I see the thought I felt in our clasped fingers.
You are mine you said.
And my eyes joyfully replied,
Yes, I am yours.
Now, as our quiet moment ends,
We take each other's hand
And stride on with the throng
Because, when we are hand in hand,
There's nothing that can go wrong.

STORY BEHIND "HOLDING HANDS"

I remember the first thing that happened as a teenager was holding hands with a boy. It was the most exciting thing to happen to me. Of all the other things to come, this first experience was totally physical and gave insight into the male species.

I remember the boy very well. He became the first boy I kissed and later our lives changed drastically. We found each other again in the United States of America, but it just was not meant to be. My family found his friendship lasted for many years as he always called at holiday time to speak to my mother and ask after me.

The years went on and one day his interest waned. Clearly, I was not going to be a part of his life.

That first impression stayed with me. So much is said in the act of holding someone's hand. You can say you are happy. You can say you are sad. You can say and you can feel what the other person is saying to you as well.

So why does it not happen so much today? Why don't we hold hands as much anymore? Phones with must-read updates have replaced the once tender act or interaction between couples. What I noticed is that even children do not hold parents' hands or siblings' hands. But the elderly hold hands. That made me look more closely at more senior couples. Their holding hands is a means of communication.

- Watch out for something harmful.
- Be mindful of the step up ahead.
- A gentle nudge to alert the other of a necessary action.
- To say, "there's a problem".
- To say, "look at this nut over here" and the shared smile or giggle.

When the younger folks do a version of hand holding, I interpret it more as a show of possession or a badge of

honor.
I simply love the comfort of holding hands.

5
THE GRAND GRANDS

THE GRAND GRANDS

we call them grand parents
grand as in grandiose
grand as in important, impressive
grand as a higher ranking and so on and so on
but do we treat them grandly
no, sadly we have put them away
many of our grands have worked
so hard to provide for their young
but find themselves locked away
no visitors no calls, they quietly live
with the memories of times gone by,
bye bye, the words they hear most
because everyone must leave to return to their own places
the grands who are blessed with the ability
to still move about on their own know a special joy
so often though it is the beginning of a new way of living
it is not continuation of the progression of a family line
as the young grow up, ties are severed and
grands must find new avenues to follow

the most fortunate grands are those who are in place still
as the new lives come into being
the grands who are called upon to be caretakers of the little
ones
both embark upon the path the ancients walked
watching the babies become men and women
these grands see teaching what they were taught
these grands are blessed with the task of helping little
minds expand
yes, times have drastically changed
but the grands learn as they teach
so the lessons are froth with post and present wisdom

STORY BEHING "THE GRAND GRANDS"

This poem rose in my heart while looking at a picture of my grandmother on my dresser. My mother has joined her and so it is now applicable to her life, also. When I wrote it, Mother was still with us.

I think we have let the importance of grands slip through our hands. It seems that today they are more a burden than a source of joy. Because I grew up with my grandmother, I know how important she was to my life. My mother was blessed to have her, when she was struck down with Poliomyelitis.

My "grand" mother became mother and father and grandparent. She molded my being. She was terribly strict. She spoiled me rotten. She loved me completely.

Yes, I understand illnesses that take grandparents away and contribute to the lack of their prominence in our lives today. I still feel that the busy lives of parents keep them away from the love that could be shared by all.

I am also aware of the fact that folks simply do not get along very well with each other sometimes. So, the children will not have the exposure. I wonder how our children will be as grandparents.

I wish that I could look down the centuries to see if grandparents even exist.

I was watching a movie recently where whatever disaster had happened, a lottery was set up for those who would be saved. The cut off was 50 years old. I envision that that same scene in a future movie the age will be 25 years old. Just kidding!

I am working on being a better grand. That's all I can aspire to for my future years.

6
A GIRL

A GIRL

There will always be a girl,
whether she is good or bad,
she will be there.

Just on the outskirts of his mind,
not waiting, just being a memory,
presenting pictures of times good or bad gone by.

Lessons to re-enact,
questions to be put to rest by his answers.
never detrimental,
observed in the right light

She becomes his silent muse.
she scolds, admonishes, tease, tickles and encourages.
she can be a reminder of his best or worst.

When he is in need of a reminder that you are his life.
yes, she is there for that mostly.

Remind yourself of the attributes you are lacking.
can you make some changes that will be
the way to pull him back from those thoughts of her?

A figment of the imagination cannot compete with
your exquisite personality.
daring to eliminate those pesky feelings of jealousy
will certainly help you to shine.

You will both find a new place to begin looking at each
other again.
a girl in every man's mind will diminish.
her memory WILL fade...

only if you stay true to keeping you on his mind.
by kind words, soft kisses, the occasional
I love you and a hug around the neck.
yes, there will always be a girl
but she is no competition for YOU!

STORY BEHIND "A GIRL"

Memories are made and are filed away because everything the eyes observe, the brain remembers.

Our day-to-day lives bring people in and out, whether the time spent is long or short. Sometimes, we find impressions of a person that simply will not remain in the closed files. It is that haunting memory that surfaces at the strangest times and simply makes you smile.

We also have the frowner memories that we can put away more quickly than the smiler memories because no one wants to entertain unpleasant thoughts.

So, this one girl stays. I wrote this and realized that I had to pen a poem for A Boy because as I read the poem again. I felt that a guy's memory would bring something different.

7
A BOY

A BOY

There will always be a boy,
whether he is good or bad,
he will be there.

Just on the outskirts of her mind,
not waiting, just being a memory,
presenting pictures of times good or bad gone by.

Lessons to re-enact,
questions to be put to rest by his answers.
never detrimental,
observed in the right light,

He becomes her silent muse.
he scolds, admonishes, teases, tickles and encourages.
he can be a reminder of his best or worst
when she is in need of a reminder that you are her life.

Yes, he is there mostly.
remind you of the attributes you are lacking.
can you make some changes? that will be
the way to pull her back from those thoughts of him.
a figment of the imagination cannot compete with
your exquisite personality.

Daring to eliminate those pesky feelings of jealousy
will certainly help you to shine.
you will both find a new place to begin,
looking at each other again.

A boy in every woman's mind will diminish
his memory WILL fade,
only if you stay true to keeping you on her mind,

by kind words, soft kisses, the occasional I love you and a
hug around the neck.

Yes, there will always be a boy
but he is no competition for YOU!

STORY BEHIND "A BOY"

So, this is the same as the story for the poem, A Girl.

Men and women are very different. Yet, in this department we are very similar. We all have memories. We all react to them in one way or the other.

We decide how we react and respond to those memories and how often we revisit those memories. Our responses can be good or bad, just like the memories themselves.

I believe that men are much more prone to pursue memories of a beloved in a deeper way because it may be more of a physical reaction. A stirring in the loins often presents a problem. Guys have to work much harder than women to constrain the actions of their bodies. So, they must walk away and shut down all the amassed feelings from that relationship.

There is a coming of age that both sexes apply to their mental state that keeps them sane as the years pass. In many cases, it seems that simply being curious, kind and caring at a distance is the way to prove that all accumulations from the memory is in its place.

The idea that you loved someone so deeply for so long and suddenly you totally hate them is hard for me. I have chosen to keep my distance but at the same time show that my humanity is still intact, no matter what transpired.

This is a self-preservation tactic, in that I believe that that destructive anger finds a way out some day. Forgive and forget is definitely not an easy task. However, over time it can be accomplished.

Besides, think of how foolish a person who has hurt you will feel when they realize that you have forgiven them. They might still hold on to the rage that caused the break. The forgiver is the better for the forgiving, which allows peace of mind and the ability to move on to the next adventure.

Life will not stop presenting situations, and we cannot walk away from them. Each action we perform takes us in another direction for better or for worse. You choose.

ARLENE McGUIRE

8
FOR LOVE'S SAKE

FOR LOVE'S SAKE

Inside us all resides the power of love.
But we never really use it.
We use the word in our expression of an emotion.
But loves full potential is often not fully known.
The heart when challenged in this arena of emotions
Often collapses as many other responses surface.
But love is usually the last to be called, if called at all.

Deep inside us resides the power of love.
And today, we should ask the heart
How to show and use this love that waits patiently there.
We can face a singular circumstance and call it up
And its arrives as a soft smile – Share it!
The heart will beat faster as this love pours forth.
It will cause you to catch your breath.
The one who needs this expression of love waits
And your joy in sharing will take you
To a place of ecstasy, with the shared kiss.

STORY BEHIND "FOR LOVE'S SAKE"

Is there a different feeling within you when you say the words I LOVE YOU? Are you saying it just because it is what we say? Or as you utter those words to someone, does the person feel anything?

As I played with the grands, I had to listen to those words as they were said and listen to the responses. Small children have no clue what the nature of the word is. As an adult, it feels totally different when those words take on a most simple tone.

How often is our love bound by strings, different lengths, thickness and strength? The next time you tell someone you love them, see if you feel any of those things.

Is there a direct line from your heart to theirs, or is the line a little frayed, worn or maybe even broken? With a broken line, I think the "you" may not be uttered at all. Immediately, the emotion floods your mind and you ponder why do you not love them wholeheartedly.

Many things can come to the fore with that question. Oftentimes we really do not want to dwell on or rehash the whys and wherefores of it all. So, we smile and put the lid back on Pandora's box. That proverbial box has many other emotions that seem to be put to use much more often than love.

The one time that there is a most joyful feeling bursting from our lips is with little children. Is it because we know that when they say I love you back, it has a purity. A purity that you can bask in, that can buoy you for hours in a day. When you think of the moment they spoke that honestly to you, your spirit soared. The gratitude you feel is real because you know that you have lost the sanctity and sacredness of that feeling.

It is still a very powerful word. Many are very afraid of it. It brings change, challenges a different beat to one's heart, a beating we crave yet fear. Some people protect themselves by not saying it because it requires a commitment, which means you are vulnerable to hurt after saying those words. It is all too funny how that word can change so much about a person.

The time I think we are safest saying it is regarding God.

A Chorus I loved to sing says:
I love you Lord, and I lift my voice
to worship you, oh my soul rejoice.
Take joy, my King, in what you hear
and let it be a sweet, sweet sound in your ear.

9
FIGHT FOR LOVE

FIGHT FOR LOVE

We have lived and loved
And now we live in fear
Fear of failing you
Fear of failing me
We have lived and loved and now
Our bodies fail us
As we stand face-to-face
We must seek and find
A new way to share our love
A glance, a smile, a blown kiss
Can regenerate our simplest form of expressing
Those three feared words... I love you!

STORY BEHIND "FIGHT FOR LOVE"

If you are married, I know that you have had to fight for love because without that fight the next feeling is giving up. For each couple, that timeline runs differently. Where it began for me was with a physical change.

Every woman's favorite thing happens and knocks it right out of the park. Yes, the dreaded MENOPAUSE. It's horrific when it manifests, mostly because we have had to live in dread for so long. We have had to listen to how much the body changes, how those around you respond to it, and how self-worth can be destroyed by it.

My mother could tell me very little about all those things because it was becoming a named event in my time. Back in the day, all the information about this time of life was limited. It was simply something that happened and women endured it.

Now, there are all kinds of medication, herbs and creams lotions and potions. Like my mother, I simply suffered through it. I did think of buying some of those things, but I knew I would not follow through with using what I bought. So, I did not spend much money on them. I cannot say with conviction if the item worked because I started out not putting much stock in it any way. It would have had to knock me down with success for me to notice. Well, that sweating still goes on. The funny thing is you begin to experience being too wet and then elsewhere you are too dry. I still don't get it.

This life change causes a chasm to develop. Husbands tease and pull away somewhat. Wives withdraw for fear of the taunts, mostly because the insipid feeling of physical contact makes some women (like myself) cringe.

In the event, a spouse or boyfriend becomes touchy feely, you simply want to run away.

When I thought about the importance of trying to overcome the feelings of fleeing, this poem came to me. I had all the assuring words I could need. I simply could not accept them and let myself relax into even the simplest embrace or hug. That hurt because I love to hug! I speak of finding a new way to ignite that loving feeling, but I did not accomplish the task. We simply dealt with our reality, and physicality became secondary even non-existent, hence the encouraging word, Fight.

Put your heads together and figure out how to put simple expressions of love back (if they are slipping away) into the humdrum everyday living. When the doldrums arrive and you feel it happening, you feel the distance growing. That is your signal to fight.

10
ARE YOU ALONE

ARE YOU ALONE

Where are you tonight,
Sitting quietly feeling a singular pain?
Your head is bowed as thoughts of lost love invade your
heart.
Your physical failure is not the end of life.
You can use it to take you to a higher place.
Entertain your being as a gift of love,
Not simply an organ of pleasure.
You can be a complete expression of love.
Become completely involved with the energy.
Become the warmth, the joy of love.
Become completely involved with your lover,
Sharing mounting passion that culminates in tears of joy,
As you both embrace a new oneness,
A stronger greater sense of a unique new you,
A sense of sharing without the pressure,
A sense of sharing with only the desire of giving.
Giving and receiving an equal sharing of mind and body
Gives you the assurance and the promise that you are not
alone.

STORY BEHIND "ARE YOU ALONE"

Mostly when this event of ED-erectile dysfunction appears in a couple's life, they experience complete and utter loneliness. There is a vast nothingness that you simply wander in day after day.

At first, it infuriates you that it is happening. Then with research, study, and medical advice, you begin to understand and accept the circumstances. The acceptance helps decrease the loneliness because now you understand that your partner may be feeling worse than you do. He is feeling alone, due to lack of the ability to take care of the physical needs. That can be a very lonely place, I'm told.

It is the least understood disease, and now that Viagra has taken over, everyone is fine. After the research I did, medicating ED is not the best thing to do on a regular basis. Like everything in life, there is a price to pay for taking the happy pill.

There is no way back from this disease and everyone goes through it, men in their way and women with theirs. Yes, women grow into a sexual dysfunction of their own. When this happens, we can now live without these feigned headaches. Or, we can now stop working late nights. If more people embraced erectile dysfunction as a new way of life, they could have more fun than ever.

I was too busy suffering to enact what I just wrote. I was too busy trying to convince my spouse that I was loyal. This event could not and would not cause me to desert him. Well, with much trial by fire, we survived this storm. On the other side, you can see yourself as a person of worth, as an individual who understands that loyalty is probably more important than love.

11
GO FISH FOR YOUR LIFE

GO FISH FOR YOUR LIFE

The lives we live are like a card game.
So often we just can't understand what's going on.
For others, it seems all is well all the time.
What we see year after year tells a different story from the
day-to-day.
Small struggles, setbacks, tragedy, loss, pain, suffering and
problems come to each of us.
Those who seem to breeze through life have their share,
and those who live in chaos, theirs.
The difference in the picture is the attitude.
With a right attitude, life can be a piece of cake.
But when we have attitudes that work in the wrong way,
mountains become molehills.
Like the card game, let's Go Fish for a mindset that
reminds us daily that no problem can overtake us.
There is always and eraser on our pencil.
We can backspace, spellcheck, and even photoshop a
situation and turn it around.

STORY BEHIND "GO FISH FOR YOUR LIFE"

I thought that was the sillies name for a card game. I still can't play that game. The title, however, makes me smile. The idea it brings is one that can be funny or mean. I choose funny. "Go fish! Get outta here! Go on 'bout your business!" That was a very old taunt. I'm not sure what the young ones say that would mean go fish today. Well maybe I can LOL.

Now, as an adult, is that not what happens in life?
We are all on a fishing trip. We are prepared with the basics and head out into the wild blue yonder of life. While the waters are sometimes choppy, most of the time we can simply enjoy the waves as they come and go. Every now and then, an occurrence causes us to sit up straight and tend to our line. There may or may not be a fish at the other end even after the hard work of trying to reel it in.

How often have we seen the sign "Gone Fishing"? Well that becomes a necessary task sometimes. Life becomes too crowded, too full of trouble and the need for the calm waters and a line are needed. I never understood that whole thing about fishing, but the years have brought the explanation.

Fishing trips can be used to accomplish many things:
- Time alone with someone.
- Making secretive deals.
- Planning undercover ops.

You get it. It is a time where the only interruption would be a fish biting your line or choppy waters causing sea sickness.

I think I will learn to play this game now that I have had another look at it regarding life.

Well, good fishing to you all.

ARLENE McGUIRE

12
DANCE OF A YOUNG
& OLD SOUL

ARLENE McGUIRE

DANCE OF A YOUNG & OLD SOUL

When we met, my mind said no.
Then you asked me to dance.

Your embrace screamed of tenderness.
My heart said yes.

Bodies ever so lightly touching, became extreme
enticement.
My mind said, "No, this is forbidden fruit."
The song had ended and so had the moment of passion.

Wait… No… We were dancing again
To a slower, softer beat now,
which keeps me pressed gently
against a powerful young body.

My mind screaming NO, resounded in my head,
Forewarning of my impending doom, if I stayed.
We linger in the embrace and sway gently to the beat,
until, there is an easy movement apart and unlocking of our
selves.

My mind is no longer forewarning.
My heart is in double time beating out a new symphony.
We went back to our separate group of friends,
paying little attention to each other across the room.

Affording quick glances at each other
to assure each other of our interest.
Still, we party on apart.
Now, some hours later, we talk quietly,
as it's the end an enchanted evening.

Ever so gently, we are reminded of the misting rain,
caressing our faces.
We come together again in a most tender kiss,
which is prolonged by a lingering caress of your lower lip.

My body seems frozen in goodbye.
No movement in my thighs begin.
The turn away from you seems to go on for hours.
I open my eyes and look at your face
and know I need to go.

Heart and mind are now in synchronized.
This, is way out of your ken.
"Ok, ok!" Putting on my best smile,
I mumble the words and turn away.
There is a quick flurry of movement
and I am in your arms again.

Not for long, a simple brushing of bodies.
Then a gentle final separation. I sit in the car.
My lower back has the warm imprint of your hand.
My ever-vigilant mind suggests, demands, entreats me:
DO NOT LOOK BACK!
My heart aches. The car is in drive. My heart is in idle,
needing one quick glance.
My voice offers up justification.
It was a dream, he can't be real.
Look back to be sure.
My mind pounds on my skull
with the wisdom of the ages.
He is too young!
I look... I die!

STORY BEHIND
"DANCE OF A YOUNG & OLD SOUL"

At some time in life, more specifically older life, a situation may arise where you find yourself attracted to a younger person. I'm not able to speak of same sex situations, but regarding the opposite sex, I am able to say a few things.

First, you will be overwhelmed, mostly because you know this is foolish. This person is simply taken at something about you in the moment. It will fade with daylight and when the alcohol wears off.

The second thing is you come to terms that your age has caused a little doubt about your attractiveness to the opposite sex. Here, you find a person who is taken by you and it allows you to feel youthful stirrings within. These are not to be taken lightly. You have not had occasion to encourage them (these stirrings) in so very long. You consciously put them to rest. Even if you did call them to muster, it would be in response to someone your age or older.

A third thing happening is the excitement of being in the presence of youth, remembering your own, a questioning of what happened to it. Another question is how well or poorly you manage yours. Then you delve into the memory playback and the recrimination or regrets, regurgitating scenes to life again. Yet, you find that the feeling of being in control is comforting. Of course you know what you are about. You are clear that this is just a moment of madness to be tolerated. That person will come to his senses when you close the door after the explanation you present about the futility of it all.

Then there is laughter by both parties separately and together at how foolish this all is. You will go your separate ways and be thankful for the experience and fond remembrances. You will begin to count the years that the relationship is still in effect, much to the satisfaction of both individuals.

It is not always about sex. Spirits can connect and nurture each other without having a physical relationship. Many make a mockery of that idea until they find themselves in it and the dawn breaks on the understanding. Unless there is a financial side to that type of friendship where it is the mainstay, and superficial, friendships of old and young can last a long time, respectfully. I can proudly say that because I have participated in that experience.

13
I THOUGHT YOU KNEW

I THOUGHT YOU KNEW

See, I loved you in a place I didn't know I had.
Life takes its toll on the heart and you must protect it
And sometimes you close the doors of all that bad loving
you've had.
You face a new beginning with every ounce of
determination you can conjure up,
Always reminding yourself, you will not allow pain to
come to you again.
There is no need or place in this new you for hurt and pain.
No more lies and shame.
Rising above those feelings helps you look deep into the
next man's soul.
No, you will not be anybody's fool.
Yes, you have taken these lessons seriously.
Now you have taken the time to make you better.
You have made the improvements to mind, body, and spirit
And you can face the possibility again.
You have looked deep inside him and decided that you
have the wherewithal to love again.
This time of loving is glorious.
This time of loving is fulfilling… Yes, you believe again…
Until you find our there is no truth.
This never-ending journey mostly ends in very
overwhelming painful lessons.
We must receive each one and use it to go on.
It is a new opportunity to be a better you.
I thought you knew.

STORY BEHIND "I THOUGHT YOU KNEW"

This poem is about recuperating from the pain of a break up. Repeated breakup even.

The mind and body are at odds when this destruction comes into a life. First, the pain rides the mind into feeling that it is not happening or hasn't happened. Reality stands up in the mirror after a while and reminds the individual that they need to come to terms with the situation and begin again. The darkness of this time is a living nightmare. You can't eat or sleep. You think your brain is stuck on one and only one thought HIM or HER! They will not get out of your head, and you are clear that they must. They are gone with someone else. Yes, you are alone.

Blindness sets in. Day becomes night. All faces and voice are one. Every voice is now one. You simply can't get past the shame, fear, hunger, or need for the missing limb. At some point, we all get to that point to say, "To hell with this!"

If this is my reality, well so be it. Or you find yourself just getting by from day to day. Numbness keeps the hurt away and you are functional, so all is well.

Years go by and then some knucklehead turns on the light and outside of that darkness you see him/her and you begin to have a very gentle movement. Or they bowl you over and you can't breathe.

Now your power of determination to not revisit that old friend disappointment steps up and reminds you of the promise you made to yourself… to not be a fool again. You must keep the brakes on, arms distance, for a long time to assure yourself that you have looked for problems under every rock. You find your resolve and begin with a standard in place. "Just go with it" is the saying today. No hopes and dreams. No expectations of longevity, just in the moment allow the other person to just enjoy being with you and you them. It's a place of sanity from which to begin, not sending messages of expectations to the other and allowing them to feel you are not holding them to any expectations.

This is where 'You Know' shows up in our actions, and allows sanity to rule, not insane hormones.

14
HE MAN

HE MAN

Now he can laugh at life.
he no longer stands in its storms
and beat his chest.
There's no need to hurl curses
at the destructive winds that bring tests,
which serve only to cause his knees to buckle.
Time marches on and finally he understands
the phenomena he calls life.
All is duality.
Each time joy is experienced,
sorrow must be expected on the horizon.
Maybe not exactly the next day,
but he learned to truly enjoy "the JOY".
During the sorrow, he can remind himself
that this too shall pass.

STORY BEHIND "HE MAN"

So often when trouble comes, our first response is why? How come this happens to me? Our singularity is in question as if we are the only person on the planet. Over time, we learn that everyone, even the person who seems to lead a charmed life, has problems.

If nothing, He Man realizes that there is nothing but acceptance in this life. We can weather the storms that come. Show patience during the sunny days and put on the brakes because more tests are on the way.

If you've ever had the experience of being on a shrink's couch, they used to count you down to sleep. A new methodology is to send you to a safe place, a familiar place where you feel peaceful. Why is that? Because there you can find yourself and really look at the absurdity of it all. Better still, you feel no compunction to hold back. This is the time you pay to be heard.

Some of us can do this for ourselves, some of us must pay for the help to survive. Wherever you fall on that line is fine. Ultimately, what we seek is clarity. So, the end justifies the means.

My saying that all is duality is my take away on life. The template I look at is how the seasons play out and where scripture states that's how He ordered it. Well, if the elements have order, humans probably need more than just order.

There was a song that said there's a thin line between love and hate. We know that to be so true with divorce. Two people who were so in love one day, stand with swords drawn in full battle armor the next. That makes me laugh as I remember pictures from the Enquirer newspaper. Their photographers back in the day somehow got pictures that showed the battling parties as sad or grief-ridden.

Today, the absolute worst pictures are published. Looks of hate are a replacement of sadness. I often wonder if they choose the worst pictures to turn you against one of the two people. Well that's a whole other story there. Moving on.

15
THE UNEXPECTED

THE UNEXPECTED

When life goes awry and the daily grind and problems
leave you cold to the touch,
the unexpected arrives and could be missed.

A quick unexpected kiss,
caress of the derriere,
a lingered press of bodies in a small place,
passing each other a look
of knowing exactly what you're thinking,
punctuated with a smile.

When eyes are studded with sleep,
the smell of a proffered cup of coffee,
to which thank you is not forthcoming
because you find your tongue tied, in delight.

These simple things are so often what we seek.
As the days become humdrum, routine, even boring,
look in your heart for a few of these unexpected things
you can give, then smile because the recipient
has to come up out of the haze
and realize you just unexpected them.

Now, they have a smile of gratitude.
As they feel your heart in that offering,
they know you have stepped out of your haze
to help bring them back to you.

Try the unexpected. Sometimes
you might like it.

STORY BEHIND "THE UNEXPECTED"

We live in the now, the everyday routine, and when the unknown occurs, it surprises us. Although those surprises come in the form of pleasant and unpleasant, I am thinking now of only the pleasant surprises.

These are the small kindnesses that we don't often think about today. Seems to me they are taken for granted and have disappeared altogether.

I wrote this upon returning home from work one morning. The night shift takes its toll on the mind and body over the years and I was very tired. As I tossed my coat into a chair, I noticed a rose on my bed. At 4 a.m., a rose is the most unexpected thing. There was nothing else, just a rose. It made me smile. I went to the bathroom and put it in a vase and went to bed.

The next day, I was so sure it was my husband that left it. I called him at work to say thank you. To my surprise, he said he had not left it. He said my son was in town and I should check the guest room. Well, I was simply overjoyed. I went to bed and didn't wake him, since I knew he had a long journey.

The next day, was full of hugs. The poem is mostly about doing a kindness for a spouse or lover, but as I began to write that memory of the unexpected rose came to me so I added it.

When relationships go on for a long time, both parties lose sight of each other. There are so many distractions today that it is much harder to stay together.

But if one member of the couple does something simple but unexpected, it puts a smile on the recipient's face. It brings them out of whatever they are dealing with and makes them see you!

So, every once in a while, I think you and I should try doing something to make someone else smile. In this instance, my son showed me love and I smiled as I went to sleep.

16
DAY'S END

DAY'S END

She sits alone at twilight.
She sits very still waiting.
There is a delicate fog,
gently surrounding her.
Her eyes see beyond looking.
She seeks his image, his familiar smile.
Amelia knows the new search.
She has begun. Tonight will end,
just as all the other nights have.
She will wake up alone.
The desire for love remembered
from so many years gone by
lives on, living every day in loneliness.
She lives her everyday humdrum life
until twilight, when day turns to evening.
Tonight, she embraces this gentle time of day,
as it sweetens her thoughts of him.
Yes, twilight heightens her senses
as she awaits the gentle warmth
of his hand on her shoulder,
the reassurance for her mind
of his love and longing.
As quickly as he appears,
he is gone.
So goes each tear,
a memory now, a sensation lingering.
She seeks sleep with the setting sun.
She lays on her bed
to sleep now and not dream.
Why? Because the fantasy
is more real at twilight.
She loves him again and again.

STORY BEHIND DAY'S END

Have you ever been her? I have. It is a very delicate place, one remembered many times down the years. It's not just a youthful thing either. Up in age, a girl can be very real in certain circumstances.

Is there a time of day you prefer? As a child, I recall my friends and I running from the beach two blocks to get home at dusk. Our mothers would be out in the yards looking down the street for us. Sometimes, we got carried away down there and they would come out to look.

Well, the beauty of that time in my childhood went away. No beaches, just the cement jungle of Harlem. But the time of day I now call twilight was beautiful. You could feel the close of the day. We had a top floor apartment and you could see more sky up there and my window had a pillow I would lean on and just look at the sky.

I became a mother quite early in my life and I recall sitting with a small baby in that window. The beauty of the sky and the beautiful baby boy in my hands made me weep.

The girl in the poem dreams of a love lost or forgotten. Yet, her mental state in that beautiful light of evening helps her feel the person who owns that love. She knows he is in another place, time. But at twilight, she can identify her feeling of closeness very quietly and as night begins she releases her memory. The time for rest comes very quietly and sleep allows her to forget, to stop remembering for today.

ARLENE McGUIRE

17
HANGING OUT IN THE QUIET

HANGING OUT IN THE QUIET

I come to the garden mostly alone.
Sometimes, the dew still feeds the earth.
I look at all those I pass.
Sometimes, I stop and have a word.
To the new folks, I wave a welcome.
My gait is slow and measured
because unlike the rest of the world
I am hanging out in the quiet.
I can feel the unseen walkers.
We have no need for words.
I come to rest on a blanket.
In the quiet, my words seem to have meaning.
My thoughts almost sprout wings and take to the sky.
No judgement here. No quarrels. No yays or nays,
Just expressing myself, releasing, receiving.
Sometimes, quite suddenly, I have nothing more to say.
I look to the sky and feel the sun's rays.
They seem to send a burst of energy.
I say my goodbyes and gather my things
With promises to return. I beg my leave
So often it feels less painful to walk away.
I look back and wonder if what I feel
Is the encouragement of them all.
Forced to listen to my stories of pending doom,
They smile now as they know
I, too, will one day know.
I am on the vast stage of life.
My best performance of my life is the requirement
Feeling the peace and joy when the curtain closes.
The applause to follow is the swan song,
The precursor to my entry into the quiet.
I will miss my loved ones no more.
They will share their garden as we await
The visitors who stop by.

Many come to talk. Many come to cry.
Some stop by to share news. Others just need to visit
And hang out in the quiet of the graveyard,
The quiet of the cemetery.
The quiet of the final resting place,
A little before their time.
See you soon.

STORY BEHIND
"HANGING OUT IN THE QUIET"

Unfortunately, my mother is at rest in a garden that is about five miles from my home. I use that highway with much frequency and have found myself jumping out into the turning lane to get into the entrance. Just a random desire strikes me and there we are.

At first, I used to be so sad. As time went on, it became a joy to stop and have a chat. The reality of life can be found in this garden. Age makes that reality more real than ever now. But it also lessens the fear. Each visit allows me to let go of the feeling that this will be a difficult place to be. I remind myself that I won't even know I'm there.

When I drive thru that garden and pass all those folks, a reverence comes over me. I used to feel that reverence in church as a child. I have grown older feeling that there is nothing revered in life anymore, except the grave yard.

Some people are afraid of being there. Others see themselves there and avoid it. Some do not want to be reminded that they, too, will end up there. At this time in my life, it's comforting to read those names and give a thought to those I pass. I have looked at dates on headstones and tried to remember what I was doing on the day so and so passed. Or, where in relation to me were they born.

Husbands and wives are the most intriguing. I read their birth dates and when they departed. Who left first? How long after one died did the other join them? You try to conjure up what they looked like and what they did in life.

Military service members are the ones I always say, "Thank you" to. They gave us so much of their life in one way or another. I don't feel I have to know them personally. They were here once and maybe they have not had a visitor in a while, so my greeting is the least I can do.

This may sound trite to some readers but here is a good story. The lady next to my mom had the same name as my paternal grandmother. I do not believe there was any love lost between those two. My grandmother was probably not happy about her son getting hitched so early in his life. Early in their marriage, my mother was diagnosed with poliomyelitis. I often ask my mom how she gets along with grandmother's namesake. It's my running joke when I sit with them.

Quiet time in the garden hurts no one. Go visit some of those folks just for the peace and quiet someday.

18
VISION

VISION

The men and women of vision down the ages have come
with strong desire to put humanity on a better path.
We've read their stories.
We've understood their dreams.
We have taken up the battle cry
and brought about drastic or quiet change.
Today, we think of Dr. Martin Luther King
and all he stood for.
We recall his departure from this life
and we say thank you for all you did.
We are in hope that another visionary
will tell our children a new story,
represent a new cause to help mankind.
This is not a race for the swift.
This is not a race to glory.
Instead, it should be a new message
that drives us to treat each other as human beings.
A message of hope from the writings of history recall the
suffering, and atrocities.
In this lifetime, we should do our utmost
to not repeat these stories in newfangled fashions in dress.
Let us seek man's humanity to man,
lifting our race instead of continuing on this path of
destruction.

STORY BEHIND "VISION"

Great men and women come and they go. Sometimes we look for greatness in the world and it is right next to us. I wrote this and thought about the family of Dr. King.

I had this poem come to me after listening to a news story about the controversy about letters Dr. King wrote. Just prior to that, his museum was in another story. It made me remember who he was and what he did.

Men and women of great vision are among us even now, waiting to step into the light and present what they have been sent to say and/or do. The idea that some of us deny those stirrings is very sad. However, we should remember those who brought great messages down through the years.

What's important is that new visionaries arise because so many need to know what they have to say. When we look at our children, we must accept the fact that each of them have a piece of greatness that will surface one day. They may need to be encouraged or schooled on a path or endeavor we know little about. We must see them through what they must do. We must be supportive of their efforts, simply because we do not know how or what impact they may have on the world. The world could be their street. It could be their Sunday school class. Good seeds have been planted and we can help them to grow. Help them to do what they have come to us to do.

19
HANDKERCHIEF

A HANDKERCHIEF

Where are they now?
Mostly fashion statements of the rich;
an old fashion accessory that had so many uses
has gone the way of the wingtip shoes,
the Bonnets, Petty Coats and Pocketbooks.

Handkerchiefs are mostly used for decoration,
embellishing and color-coordinating an outfit.
What has been lost is the subtle use
for handkerchiefs for men and women.

Ladies carried them, perfumed to stave off unpleasant
smells, to dab a tear or stop a sniffle.
It would be casually dropped to catch a gentleman's eye.
He would be courteous and return it
at which time an introduction was made.
Gentlemen were chivalrous and if a lady was upset,
he could offer a way to prevent tears from falling.

The lady would have an excuse, or
let's call it an opportunity, to return it and make said
gentleman's acquaintance.
I will venture to say people today look out for ways to
hookup via text messages.
Today, it seems casual sex is the next step after hello.
I guess the good old days of
getting to know you are long gone.
I hold to the fact that those days were more challenging,
just like a man with a pocket handkerchief.

Often the simple exchange of, 'Thank you', could start
fireworks in the heart of a man and a woman.

STORY BEHIND "HANDKERCHIEF"

I wrote this poem after watching a movie in which a scene reminded me of when I met my husband.

It took me back to when I first met my husband. He always had a handkerchief. He still does and if I have a hot flash, he gently nudges me and offers it.

Handkerchiefs are needed when hot flashes refuse to subside. So, he just made that a way to help me. In the movie, the woman was crying about the loss of a friend. A guy out of nowhere showed up with the life-saving hanky. How cool was that? No one else had one, didn't think to offer it or just did not care. All I know is this guy saved the day. No running mascara or smudged eyeliner. Thank goodness.

I recall Mae West in scenes and she always had a handkerchief. Actually, most of the old movies had them as part of the wardrobe, I think. They were so commonplace, a thing in life that they disappeared unnoticed.

Paper tissues (Kleenex) became the replacement for which we spend far more money than we did for handkerchiefs. I still can't stand paper towels and tissues. When you dab sweat, it leaves those embarrassing dots on your skin. Then, as it dries, you feel it and try to get it off your face.

That was the cool thing about handkerchiefs; they didn't leave pieces on your face. Why did we think using paper to wipe our face would be better than a soft piece of absorbent cotton? I don't know.

Then there is the scenario I like where you can have a very quiet introduction to a guy that you might like with the interaction of receiving an offered hanky. Or returning a hanky you were given on some occasion. The thank you opened the door to an introduction and who knows what else. Well, I can't remember any situations in my life where that happened. And now it won't happen because I hate

paper towels and tissues, so nobody better offer me that.
I'm just kidding. I would be more than happy to accept
help.

20
DREAMS OF YOUTH

DREAMS OF YOUTH

During my lifetime, I have witnessed…
No, we have witnessed how age is assessed or
How age has acquired new lines of demarcation.

My teens meant I could go to a party until 11 p.m.
I could date a boy my parents liked.
A light application of lip gloss was ok.
Eye shadow on a very special occasion.
On all other days, Vaseline was your moisturizer.

Being openly provocative was a prohibited.
Dresses worn above the knees were verboten.
If you did wear clothing with much of your body exposed,
You were scolded by the head shaking, cut eyes and
The tsk tsk of the lips.

All too often, an elder would take you aside
With strong admonitions.
Fashion dictates covered those short dresses and skirts
With maxi coats.
Baggy pants were the only appropriate way to dress.
I played by the rules as best I could,
But still found myself in trouble or trouble found me.

A few years passed and adulthood was upon me.
I had to pay bills. Little mouths needed to be fed.
I found myself asking,
'Where did the days of youth disappear to?'
Many more years have come and gone and
It is clear that the days of youth were the most important.
They were to be lived. The challenges they brought should
not be hidden from.
A sheltered youth provides no fodder for growth.
Often, the wild-eyed stare of a burgeoning adult

Is indicative of fear, a lack of knowledge for application
To life's circumstances. Now that I get it,
Why is it that I did the same foolish protective behavior
To my children, only to find I shielded them from nothing?

Things still happened to them and we survived so
I have advice for them... Stop dreaming about your youth.
It is now grown and gone.
Give your children safety and allow them to venture out
Into the great big world and find their adventures.

They will get knocked down and bruised
But every scab that heals becomes a life lesson.
Those dreams of youth can now become anecdotes
For everyone and we will raise our glass
To the dreams of youth.
Long live you!

STORY BEHIND "DREAMS OF YOUTH"

I'm sure you can guess the reason I wrote this one. Fleeting youth comes upon me as I rest my head on the pillow, with the thought that it was too fleeting, grinning in the dark! Now, the remembrances are equal to a ball swung at and missed in a baseball game. The look on the batter's face is like "Damn, that was fast. Where did it go?" Well, youth moves at the same speed as that fast ball, right by your head.

Yes, now I find myself in the reminiscing state, looking at my youth, especially when there are old pictures around. I believe this poem came into being as I started building my first collage on a 11x7 board. This thing is a lot of work. After finishing the first board and sitting and looking at my life in these pictures, I was taken aback at it all.

All the events in a life were laid out by pictures. The stories behind them were known only to those who were part of it. But the person whose life it is, gets to recall so many things, places, and people. It can be dizzying fun, but can also bring sad stories and memories because every life has both sets of circumstances in different ways. Each of us must play the part we came with.

I recollect all the things my parents told me and the guidance they provided but I had my own way to go. My playbook read a little different from theirs. As parents, we run these plays thinking we will make all the difference in the world only to watch our children grow up and do what they have to do. It's not for lack of effort that I tried to drum into my children what was drummed into me. But ultimately everybody goes to their corner, towel off and return to center ring. That's how it goes.

Youth is to be embraced when young. Youth is for pushing the boundaries, the envelope and testing one's mettle. But as a parent, I still cringe watching these little people learning to walk, run, ride a bicycle, or a skateboard. I'm losing my mind with fear about the scars and pain they will end up with. Now, I can laugh at myself about this because these things are to be endured. It makes for great storytelling at Thanksgiving dinner.

21
HAIKU POEMS

HAIKU POEMS

I.
wool over your eyes
star that brings the light of night
truth comes with the dawn

II.
early life eyes wide
now in the winter of life
eyes do close daily

III.
I am too wise now
through the long winters of life
to love you this way

IV.
young old yin and yang
each season brings with it love
old young then yang yin

V.
passion knocks gently
thunder darkening blue skies
bold and bare we lay

VI.
big blue skies shimmer
summer's vivid hues abound
mirrored skies my waves

VII.
fear can hold the soul
as winter's icy fingers
only until spring

VIII.
the joy that dawn brings
beautiful fruit blooms begin
summers new journey

IX.
to sleep and to dream
of a winter without snow
days waiting for night

X.
the art of waiting
aids the growth of your true grit
timely smiles endure

XI.
we take for granted
the gifts of sunshine and rain
soul searching brings change

XII.
thoughts of you so strong
a blizzard pummels my face
tears soothe burning eyes

XIII.
hardship and tough times
walls of dark water rising
knees in submission

XIV.
unkept promises
volcanic avalanches
sorry cannot mend

XV.
can you feel my voice
as snowflakes gently touching
kisses for your ears

XVI.
superficial friends
falling snowflakes turn to shush
bold footsteps regained

XVII.
sweating means engaged
as dew on a window pane
a sacred moment

XVIII.
defining moments
tornadoes rip the landscape
a turning of hearts

XIX.
teach me of new love
first winters snow sighs
warm bodies entwined

XX.
sacrifices made
celebrating the struggles
today we give thanks

XXI.
a soul comes at death
cooling summer rain greeting
you can start over

XXII.
lose love to know love
decipher the Mojave
green pastures beckon

XXIII.
time spent comparing
winter and summer alike
live in the present

XXIV.
leaves collect the dew
gently spring rain nourishes
diamonds glistening

XXV.
feel a kiss coming
as hot rain to the sidewalk
lips evaporate

XXVI.
she stands there breathless
searching the wind for that sound
no, that's not his voice

STORIES BEHIND THE "HAIKU POEMS"

This was my first attempt at writing Haikus. Back in school, they came up as a part of our poetry classes. However, they seemed daunting to me so I put them away. The desire rose again after I joined "ighcoo the art of short verse" page on Facebook.

The rule I try to abide by is the 575.
Today many people write Haiku without holding to that rule. To me you are writing something else. The challenge of voicing your idea thought or feeling within those very strict beats for each word is not as simple as those three lines look.

So, I would find myself in the doctors waiting room writing them about whatever. I know that I only have a pretty short time to convey the idea I have in these three lines before I am called in. We don't need pencil and paper any more, I can recite the lines I have thought of into my phone. I can stop where ever because it will be right there when I go back to it. If I had to keep track of a piece of paper, well you know. So, I am thankful for the wonders of the iPhone.

The fact that we are now saying words by using letters is so funny to me. I realize that writing a haiku poem is a problem for many people. It presents the challenge of pinning down a thought with just so many syllables for each line. Who needs that, when the letters will do just fine.

So, haiku is probably considered a lost art today.

22
SHORT VERSES

SHORT VERSE #1

Laughter is as a song sung with angels.
The painful tears we shed go from our eyes
directly to the ears of God.

When my heart weeps upon being broken,
my smiling spirit reminds me
that this too shall hurt less...soon.

Hold me until I let go forever.
Winter's icy fingers melt away. So does my existence.
My next breath is not promised,
therefore I will use the forthcoming
to speak your name into continued life.

Look inside your heart to bring the miracle of you
to the night sky.
See your own blue moon in the heavens.
Feel its message deep inside you.
Let it remind you of how
astonishingly glorious you are
and shine on.

Facing oblivion with you,
tornadoes touch down silent and devastating.
I am alone again.
I'm a bent willow and I may cry
but I know I won't break.

Living life daily, I have begun to feel as if life is
the greatest magic trick of the ages.
All you were told as you grew up was not true.
As all you've learned fades away
and becomes a great lie,
all there is now as you face the closing curtain

is the dream of a new being.

If you string me along, I'll be your guitar.
Summers heat baits winter's cold.

Place a hand upon my breast, sunshine kissing snowflakes
love changes melting hearts like logs aflame becoming
ashes.

My body is yours. Ask of it what you will. We can still put
yours and mine together and make music once more.

SHORT VERSE #2

Kisses & Roses, Chocolate & Champaign
With these things you can win my heart again and again.

Quickly moments define, tornadoes tear landscapes apart.
Hearts turn to each episode.

Teach me of new love first snow of winter nights' whisper
warm bodies intertwined.

Laughter is as a song sung with angels.
The pain of tears go from our eyes
directly to the ears of God.

Soul Talk is the conversation where truth is all there is,
a touching devoid of deception.
The need for open honesty is presented and returned.
No hidden agendas, no need for lies.
The purity and simplicity shared is far stronger
and deeper than love.

Soul talking is a sharing of thoughts without words.
Soul talking is a giving without motive.
Soul talking is a simple candle always lit.
Touching the other requires a simple thought,
a memory that brings a smile which is felt across
or just there across the room.

We do not learn from the experiences of the aged among
us.
Their stories are what they were taught.
We learn by our own ability to say, "I Know".

What joy lies in the recesses of your heart brings it into the light of day.

Now consider how you can use your joy to make someone
smile, to make thousands smile.
One of those smiles will be encouraged to put their passion
to work because of a smile and a word of encouragement.
It is a simple gift so often overlooked
Smile more.

STORY BEHIND "SHORT VERSES"

These short verse poems, as with the Haiku writing, began after submission to the page on Facebook. The reviews/comments from other writers about the Haiku encouraged me.

So often, a few verses would bounce around in my head but I couldn't go anywhere with it. I would write it down and say the ending would come soon enough. Sometimes it didn't. But upon reading what I wrote, I had a feeling of fulfillment. I didn't want to say anything else. That is how these short verses came into being for me.

I find them touching to my spirit. Often, I finish reading and try to see more words that I could add. To my surprise, they convey the feeling I had and nothing added would make it any better.

My endeavors at both types of writing has given me a great deal of enjoyment.

The thought of taking a writing class has surfaced quite often. I know how I loved words as a child. I know I was taught that communication is the greatest weapon one can have. I forced myself to read the biggest books, the hardest books, and the longest books as a young person.

I did the same thing with words. The challenge was to learn the longest one and then the small words would be a breeze. Supercalifragilisticexpialidocious was the most fun thing in the world. This made me a very weird child to those around me. I had no idea it made me seem strange. All I knew was it was fun. The dictionary was the most fun book to me. Who didn't want to know what words meant and how to spell them. So that skill with words makes short verses and haikus fun.

Short verse on the other hand can encompass a few ideas that meld together. So, if my thought goes on and on and still makes sense, I rewrite to be concise. For example, a short verse begins because a butterfly alights on my hand just outside my car window. That amazes me. Simple things like a butterfly coming to rest on my hand, move me and the words come to mind creating a poem. But as I begin to replay it, I find I chose a verse or a poem.

The butterfly in all its glory shared with me a moment in time. The universe acknowledged me by that brush of its wing.

I'm reminded of the glory and power of His might by that exquisitely beautiful butterfly as it touched me that day.

23
LOVE SCENE

LOVE SCENE

As I watch a love scene play on the screen,
I wonder why we as everyday people are not given Oscars.
Are we not as good as the naked bodies on screen,
Touching, moaning through turbulent gyrations
the scene requires?
In my chair, I observe without flinching.

"Am I dead?" I quietly ask myself.
"Oh no! Not dead, just devoid of feeling."
"Ha! That's a kind of dead," I mutter back.

Now, in this scene, I feel the heat and am convinced.
I could play it even better than the actors on film.
"Yes," says the lonely member of the peanut gallery.

STORY BEHIND "LOVE SCENE"

I know you are guilty of this, too. Of course, we could play that part better. Always. But the truth is we are not all called to do so on stage. We must make our stage the ones we live in.

The day-to-day demands for pleasure never stop. So, the Oscar winning actors come to the room and begin their lines and progress to the physical engagement toward pleasure.

What happens here, however, is that pesky headache. The absolutely untimely back ache. These are the ploys that bring our Oscars because being convincing is a must so we play the part with finesse.

Sometimes, the other party is convinced, sometimes not.

Selfishness plays a big part in whether you get away with the lame excuses or not. Upon arising are you smiling in the bathroom mirror, saying mission accomplished? You know you did not intend to go through that foolishness with this person. Plus, you have a big meeting this morning. This is our truth.

Many of us know this truth and we step up proudly when our names are called to receive that award.

To me, that is exactly what should happen. Here's why. They know you were acting. They know that you know they were acting and are still inclined to applaud you for accomplishing the turning off of their desire.

So over the years, you can stop pretending and going through the motions and be honest that you simply cannot perform tonight.

Ok, maybe I should address this later.

24
A BAD ED DAY

A BAD ED DAY

I've been told that weeping may endure for a night
But joy comes in the morning.
Well it has not. I can see the early brush strokes of dawn
But I can also feel the dried
Rivulets of my tears.
I'm without energy, without drive
As unrequited lust beats a
Constant rhythm in my loins.
How do I face another day?
The need grows stronger every day,
So I wait for you.
I face today with a new mindset.
I will face this need in my body and
Use that energy to fuel my soul today.
Maybe tomorrow you'll release me with your love.

STORY BEHIND "BAD ED DAY"

As the erectile dysfunction problem took hold of my mind, I had to vent by writing. These are the words I wanted to say out loud. I thought them unkind, or they would be misinterpreted. I wrote one for the day and one for the night.

This tells you that living with ED is a 24-hour task that requires a great deal of love. The challenge of that event in life can make you weak in the knees. It hits you right between the eyes and drops you to your knees.

How does the body shut down this way? This is the one activity that life is dependent upon to be satisfying. How in the name of heaven can a person look their partner in the eyes and know that they are no longer of use in the most intimate part of life?

Well, if you are in the throes of it as you read this, my retrospective is quite simple. If you know it is an event you will be living in someday soon, same deal. After living it for so many years, here is my synopsis.

If your relationship began on the sole premise of sex, your life now requires some serious work. If your relationship began as a friendship, the loss of sex won't be too devastating. It can go either way with this loss of intimacy. In each case, there is only one saving grace, conversation... open and frank, truthful conversation.

The next thing to do is go to the doctor. The problem is when the doctor recommends a head shrinker, (I love saying that), I think of heads on a stick in rituals. Who wouldn't run at the thought of that?

The thing is both parties must understand that there is a need to talk about what is happening. In the past, there were no shrinker visits, but today we are smarter and many people go to that dreaded couch.

Much of the feeling I expressed in these poems is that giving more to each other was very important with this event, learning new ways to physically communicate. ED opens a new door to enter a new physicality, new explorations of likes and dislikes of exciting adventures that were maybe considered kinky before. Now, they are among the ways to turn things on again.

The most important thing is learning about our bodies. We become complacent about these vessels of beauty and pleasure. Now, learning more about touching and giving and taking breeds a whole new meaning. But it must be embraced by both people.

My first thought or suggestion was a walk in the park to just be together. Next, I thought of a little time of meditation together.

25
A BAD ED NIGHT

A BAD ED NIGHT

I toss and turn.

I fight my pillows and tuck my covers.

You are not here.

I'm counting sheep.

I'm counting shepherds.

I fall asleep and dream.

You are there and you hold my hands.

The stars are shining brightly.

And we bask in the moonbeam.

The shelter of your arms replaced my bed.

You put me back now.

You rest my head and kiss my cheek

I awaken to a brand new day.

Tomorrow will be here soon enough.

STORY BEHIND "A BAD ED NIGHT"

The story to A Bad ED Day applies here as well.

Nighttime, however, brought its nightmares and the awful feeling of incompleteness. These are the times I think couples should lose sleep and talk. They should dance in the kitchen until they are tired enough to go right to sleep. The cup of tea ritual would serve as together time. But I'm sure most folks would suggest a cocktail. Well, ok, if you must. Here is a place though where alcohol will not be useful. The ability to think clearly and converse and or other types of physical interaction may be more fun if sober.

ARLENE McGUIRE

26
A PERSONAL SEXUAL REVOLUTION: SEX AFTER ED

A PERSONAL SEXUAL REVOLUTION
SEX AFTER ED

How do I convince you that sexual satisfaction is still a
possibility?
Can I contrive a scenario in which fulfilment on a higher
level is possible?
Today you are a stallion.
Tomorrow you won't be in the race.
If you challenge your mind to experience the gift of
physical love,
You will continue to win the race.
Let's begin the renewing of your mind.
Begin by seeing in your mind's eyes the body you are in
love with.
Create new thoughts of sensing, feeling, touching, smelling
holding.
Create a desire to feel your lover's response to your gentle
titillation of her being.
Attempt to shut out any thoughts of sex.
This is how you begin to appreciate and find a new
type/way of loving.
Move in your mind to hearing the moans, the groans, and
sighing.
You are speaking a different language, not one of demands,
But one of adoration. This new speech is appreciation for
you still being there.
This new communication can consist of words,
not words to drive physical motion, but
Words that tell the story of your heart.
The new story of how much you need to be loved and to
give your love, not just your sexual prowess.
There are deeper stirrings you are feeling now.
Pursue them without the aggravation of needing to
experience the oh so overrated orgasm.

STORY BEHIND
"PERSONAL SEXUAL REVOLUTION
SEX AFTER ED"

Clearly, I am writing two books in one.

I had no idea that this was going to happen. I truly put that book away for another day. So, as we explore the stories that go along with these poems, I will include them here.

They are truly what I experienced as I wrote that or attempted to write that book.

I had some other far-reaching ideas that would accompany it, e.g. a meditation CD that couples could begin their journey by being together without the desire for sex.

Personally, after having lived with this illness, it has opened my eyes to so many small areas of life that are missed on the day-to-day grind.

For example: Do you know why your significant other prefers one fruit over another? Have you any idea why he will only use one brand of toothpaste? Let's reverse this. Does he know why you do?

What I discovered was that, more time was spent speaking of other simple things in life when the silence due to the lack of sex drove us mad. If a veteran is in your life, you may find that the telling of sea stories can become a mainstay for silly talks. So often you will find that you have heard that story already, many times over. However, the listening is different now. The story takes on a more real form because you have no other agenda in your mind, and are truly responding with gut-wrenching laughter. Afterwards, you find that you are tired and a hug and a kiss is all you can muster. Lights out and another day without the burden of ED is ended.

You may find that you look forward to meeting the next day with all its challenges because today you were victorious.

Of course, we know that there are so many other avenues to be traveled on this journey dealing with ED. The medical field will have you believe Viagra is the answer. I believe we are the answer. We can share ourselves and the sexual side of life can be secondary. Yes, secondary to all the other joys of life.

27
A TOUCHING ENCOUNTER

A TOUCHING ENCOUNTER

The gentle touching embrace,
wrapping arms around each other,
caressing the back of the neck.
Press the palms down to the shoulders.
Press the palms down the arms.
Connect the fingers, clasping softly.
Unclasp each finger slowly.
Emphasize the pressing of each fingertip.
Slowly open your eyes and lean back
without moving the hips or fingertips.
Feel the smile. Let it open your lips slowly.
Feel the sheer pleasure of this.
Stare into each other's eyes.
Allow your eyes to express how good your body feels
in that moment.
You may find that as you lean into each other
and step away, all you needed to say has been said.
The relaxed frames now move to the next thing
you wanted to do.
Now I ask you, where are the words?
Did you feel the need to use them
or were you really telling all you needed,
just by a simple embrace?

I believe ED can retrain us to simplify our lives.
I believe we can learn to love and express said love
without demands for physicality.

STORY BEHIND
"A TOUCHING ENCOUNTER"

ED is a crippling and sad life event. We base so much of our existence on sexuality that even conversing about not being sexually active because of ED becomes taboo.

My idea to combat ED is simple interactions that keep the humanity and stable feelings of love alive.

The reality is everybody faces it at some point. Being able to go back mentally and physically to "the old days of courtship" could help a couple interact more deeply with each other.

No demand for sex changes the way the partner is observed. I believe ED can help people to look at each other as an experiment in selflessness.

This poem asks that we react to the feeling that comes with touching, such as the softness of sharing bodies, breathing, bodies alive as the heart beat intensifies with the next anticipated touch.

Bodies get to know each other at a stronger yet softer place. Close touching ONLY encounters, meaning, "I will give you my all out of undemanding love."

28
AWAITING THE NEW YEAR

Awaiting the New Year

Quietly she sits on her bed
Dressed to the 9s
With no place she wants to go
With no one she wants to be with.
This is a night that has come and gone
Many, many times before.
She smiles and thinks of the gratitude in her heart
How long a journey she's been on,
How fast the time flew by.

Recounting the past pains and pleasures,
All filed neatly away
Because now...
She sits down to write a new chapter.
Her reflection catches her attention.
She hears Billy Crystal saying,
"You look Marvelous Darling."
She turns to stare at the mirror.
Not smiling, not reveling, simply observing
All that figure has withstood.
The skirmishes, the trips to hell and back.

Yet, what she sees in this quiet moment
Is her exquisite warrior form.
She stands erect now,
Experiencing the strength of her better self,
Her stronger self, her determination
To face the foes to come.
She assures herself with a taunting smile
That she is ready.
Her armor is ready for dressing.
The moment where her last words of gratitude go UP.
The clock strikes DOWN, to ONE.
The New Year is Now

She raises her glass to the world.
Assured, that yes, this New Year
Holds all New surprises,
That she is able to receive,
That she is able to handle.
To her reflection she says
With a whimsical smile
And raised glass,
"L'chai am!
To life!"

STORY BEHIND "AWAITING THE NEW YEAR"

The past four years have changed me drastically, due to the loss of my mother in December 2012. I have also lost the excitement and expectancy those around me share.

As the numbers stating our age grows, I think I've begun to really examine their true meaning. A reality check comes with each year and this 2016 was really important.

After my retrospective, I came away feeling I had more to do. The passing of a dear friend and the father of one of my sons was heart wrenching. His wife asked me to read a poem he had written. I was so moved at her request.

Upon taking the podium and looking out at the audience, I gulped a dry breath. The auditorium was full of guests. I believe he would have been pleased.

As I returned to my seat, I began to feel what shook me, the realization that fame and fortune are fine if you have it or achieve it. However, it should not be the goal of life, as I believed it to be for so long.

My thought was how wonderful to see and hear how the individual laying before us touched lives. No, he was not rich or famous, but this room was full of people who loved and respected him. They were now deeply saddened by his departure.

His life, presented now in death was my reminder that when god changes a life, his power and his might bring a new being into existence.

This poem was written on the night of New Year's Eve. As my grands lay sleeping, I thought about my life. I had no resolutions to make or break. I had a new drive to get back out there in 2017 and fight. I was ready to begin again to fulfill my dream and nothing would deter or distract me.

I felt my accomplishments to date were the beginning. There was more to do. There's a helping hand I can offer. There's comfort I can bring to someone through the sound of my voice. So, my lonely reflection in that mirror did not scare me; I have been all alone all my life.

So, a feeling of self-acceptance happened in those quiet hours just before 2017 took its place in my life. I had a renewed assurance that the year would bring its trials and tribulations and I would face them all down. I will rise to face each and every foe because I can. I've been at these skirmishes for a while now. I truly believe age has absolutely nothing to do with what I can put my mind and heart to and accomplish.

So, as you read this, stand with me and begin now to believe in YOU. Your purpose awaits your efforts at fruition. Begin this year to take every action to realize your dreams and purpose.

Go after it! Give it your all! Year from now, you will see that this new energy you exerted was at the right moment in time.

ARLENE McGUIRE

29
NO SUN

ARLENE McGUIRE

NO SUN

Life has offered me defeat.
I've accepted every one.
In time, I believed those lessons.
Success was not for me.
In poverty, you have one goal –
Work hard each day and dream of a better life.
Efforts tossed down and trodden into the dirt.
Dreams torn apart because you've not learned
The hypocritical smiles that lead you
To believe you'll get a helping hand,
As you are escorted out the back door.
Once again, another year goes by.
You are left with bitter gall on your tongue.
You stand at the crossroads.
You just can't go on.
There is no sun.

STORY BEHIND "NO SUN"

Sunshine sustains us. It is the most invigorating element on the planet. How often have you felt the rays of the sun make you feel alive? Or, how wonderful does a trip to the beach make you feel, after being in the sun, water and sand?

Times change and our disposition is not so sunny. We all experience the doldrums of winter. Fall is invigorating, but foreboding at the same time, due to the thoughts about the coming harshness of winter.

Life has the same seasons to it. In some lives, however, it seems as if winter is the most dominant season. The cold harsh events of life seem to shut out the sun. I believe many depressed people can't see their way forward. Medicine is not enough. Sometimes getting a person outside in the sun, can make all the difference in the world.

I guess no one can expect life to simply flow like a wandering brook that has no rocks in its path. I don't believe there is such a brook. A rough and tumble life bereft with disappointment, is often how the strongest and bravest individuals are made.

It's been said that people who are born with silver spoons in their mouths have lives to be envied. Looking back at some of the lives I have known, that does not always hold true.

In my situation, it feels as if this hill I climb is never ending, even in my later years. There is not a day that I am not fighting about something. I should stop but trials, tribulations, disappointments, and failure must happen to experience the life of ease with a grateful heart.

So, you and I need to continue knowing that a little bit

of our own personal sunshine is coming our way. All we
need to do is keep tip-toeing over the rocks in the water,
and get to the shore.

30
INSTEAD

INSTEAD

Hold me close, keep me warm.
Your heat is what I need
To keep this feeling of nothingness at bay.
Whether it's a new place or old,
We can experience it so
Our love will not grow cold.
In sickness and in health, we promised not to part
This is just a road less traveled on this road of life,
Yet a new place in our heart.
Instead of hiding, I'll hold you close.
Instead of running, I'll stand next to you in this battle.
Each day we must fight this monstrous foe.
To succumb in anger cannot be the solution,
So let us use tenderness, kindness, gratitude and love
To make the battles of our tomorrows bearable.
The victory will be ours because instead we chose LOVE.

STORY BEHIND "INSTEAD"

Here is a relationship on sputter. Last gasps of needed H2O. Let go or hold on tighter. That decision is based solely on what's in the heart.

I believe I wrote this poem at a time of dire circumstances. I believe it was exactly what I needed to remind my partner about the commitment we made long ago that was still in effect. The fight for the union can't be abandoned at the first shot across the bow.

That's the time to arm ourselves with the reminder of why we are together. It was not a casual decision. It is where the battle can be won by simply putting down the ammunition and weapons. If there was a real desire to prove to the witnesses and the creator then that poem should be indicative of my heart.

Today self-preservation is more the law of the land. The divorce rate has skyrocketed.

Folks no longer take wedding vows seriously. They are words for the moment of glory and when tough times come, the door is thrown open for departure.

So often today, I watch people who give up a year of saying I DO. What, exactly, were you DOING?

It seems that the sanctity of the union of marriage has been replaced with glitz, glitter and debt. So often the cost of a wedding becomes part of the divorce proceedings.

Somehow couples no longer fight to get to the root of issues. Instead, they would rather give up and walk away. But we must return to the matters of the heart, even in times of darkness.

ARLENE McGUIRE

31
MEN'S POEM

ARLENE McGUIRE

MEN'S POEM

I have learned to love you more each day.

As the years have come and gone,

Now, all I think of is how to stay away.

My heart breaks at my inability to speak

Of this failure of my physique.

Over and above the physical failure,

My heart breaks at my inability to speak

To speak of the burning desire I have each day.

But I can only send it away

To speak of the magnitude of my failure,

To speak of the pain behind your eyes.

Yes, to speak to you of the kisses we should share,

My heart breaks at my inability to share.

Will you hear me when I say I love you now?

Will you accept my embrace?

Is there a way to voice words I cannot find?

Can we still go on?

Can we continue to hold each other, dear?

Will our love prevail in this valley of the shadows?

Will tomorrow be a brighter day we can still share?

STORY BEHIND "MEN'S POEM"

In my opinion, this is what women want men to say to them. When the cards fall after a dispute, I think most women want to hear these words.

Sometimes, 'I am sorry' is not enough. Sometimes, I want to hear that you understand all that has gone wrong, that who you are to me is not simply dependent on this thing called love. It has to do with your hurt when I am hurt, be it intentional or unwittingly.

When disharmony comes, I know it is very difficult to talk to a woman. However, there are times after the steam blows off, that a simple reference to how badly you feel makes the sting diminish. A full-blown apology is not always necessary immediately, just an expression of your pain about the situation, of how this rift has impacted you. Men often draw a complete blank in this regard.

I feel women should encourage men to express these desires during fun conversations or easy chatter to tell of that desire and to express what you are missing because you are mad.

32
PRAYER

PRAYER

What is the best part of life?

The horror of it all at its best.

Trials, tribulations, disasters.

Sadness, pain, anguish.

Hatred, anger, loss, death.

These are the emotions I have had to label the spice of life,

Year after year, in some form or fashion.

The everlasting depletion of energy.

The waves of depression that must be beaten back daily

To find the wherewithal to go on is as

Mount Everest, the Mojave. No, not Cancun.

These are the principalities and powers of darkness

That come to one's life.

We know that the power of prayer is all we have.

On a daily basis, these terrorizing emotions and events

That bombard us can only be circumvented by prayer.

STORY BEHIND "PRAYER"

I was christened in a Catholic Church and given the name Theresa. I have not worshiped there but I love the beads that denomination uses.

Somehow, I believe that just touching them and reminding yourself that someone hears your simplest prayer must be awesome. I think I will still purchase a rosary one day.

Often as I pray, thoughts interfere and I forget the prayer. By the time I remember what I was praying, the request or thought is lost. I know it will come back and another opportunity will present itself. So, no worries.

But I wonder if using the rosary allows you to be concise in the thing you are praying for. It is expressed and you move to the next need with another need.

To answer the opening question from the poem, there is no best part of life. It is all wonderful. Just living is the best thing ever. As I wrote the good and bad things, I feel how real those things are. The not so pleasant things can bring you to your knees. And it seems that the places where you find joy are few and far apart. Sometimes they cannot even be experienced because of leftover disaster memories hanging around.

However, traveling those hills or mountains then resting in those valleys is the way life unfolds sometimes. As we learn and grow from the plethora of experiences, we become wise. With that wisdom under our belt, the drastic harshness of the events of life can be dealt with, with a certain finesse or knowing.

I believe the most important lesson everyone comes face-to-face with is that no circumstance lasts forever. The length of time may seem endless, but it is not. When it ends and we look back, it is usually surprising that we didn't suffer as long as we thought. But it sure did not feel like it.

ABOUT THE AUTHOR

Arlene McGuire grew up in Harlem, New York, with her family who all came to the US from Jamaica, West Indies. As a young person, she loved words, including reading and writing essays, which allowed her mind to take flights of fancy and sharing for others to enjoy. In addition to her dream of being a writer, Arlene desired to be a voiceover artist, which she achieved as a podcast narrator in the Vertikal Reading Room. She also does radio drops on The Urban Sound Suite on Black Country Radio; The Jumpstart Show on Twilight Soul Radio in the UK; and Online with DJ Matt Houston. In her spare time, Arlene enjoys painting and spending time with her grandchildren. She and her husband reside in the Atlanta area.

FOR MORE TITLES FROM EX3 BOOKS

VISIT OUR WEBSITE AT:
www.EX3BOOKS.com

Feel free to leave reviews about
Hanging Out in the Quiet
on our website, email info@ex3books.com, or
at Amazon.com.

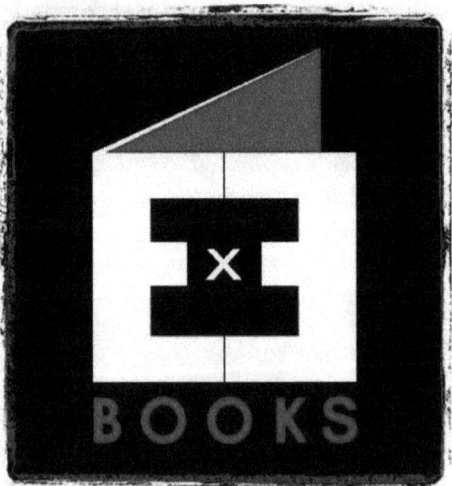

www.ingramcontent.com/pod-product-compliance
Lightning Source LLC
Chambersburg PA
CBHW051840090426
42736CB00011B/1895